UNHEALED HEART

The Molesting Hands

TANYA JEFFERSON

Unhealed Heart

The Molesting Hands

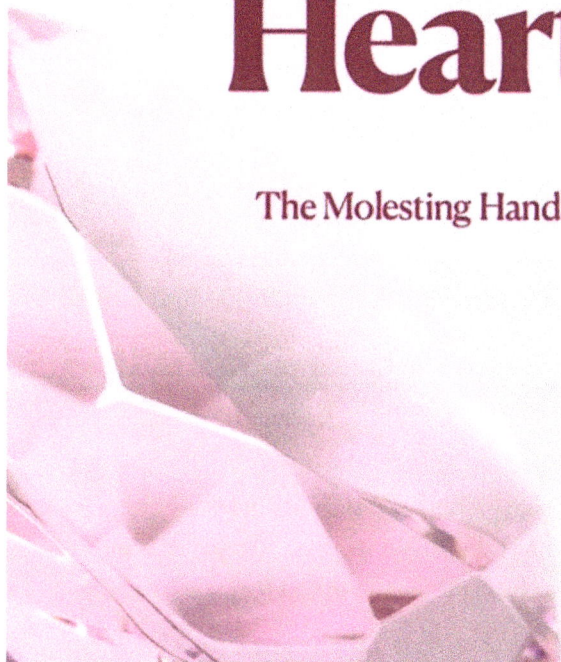

I offer this book to you, my Lord and Savior Jesus Christ, the true and living King.

You know that this is something that my flesh did not want to do. You told me to jot down my memories. You told me to jot down my thoughts and it was so therapeutic; but when you told me to write the book, my nerves, fears, and all of my doubts surfaced to the forefront. I didn't know that the words would just come. I didn't know that this was truly apart of deliverance...for me! You know that my flesh fought against this, but my soul says "Yes, Lord." I want what You want.

So I dedicate this book to you. My one true love. To the one that wiped every tear from my eyes. To the one that comforted me when I thought all hope was lost. To the lover of my soul and the author and finisher of my faith. Just like my life, I dedicate this to you, Jesus. I learned to call on your name while I was a baby on the pews. I heard your name in every prayer that my mother prayed. I heard your name in every message that my father taught. I heard your name slip from my lips even when I drifted away, and I've seen you come to my rescue. I dedicate this to you, my great defender. Give me the words to say to convey the sentiment of my heart: You are the purest form of love. You are the love that my heart longs for.

Acknowledgments

Where would I be had it not been for the Lord who woke me up from slumber? I thought that my childhood dream of being an author was dead, but God has a way of waking up the very thing that you thought was deceased.

I thank you, Jesus for holding my hand during this process and causing me to push past fear, rejection, and the opinions of others.

I'd like to say thank you to my loving and supportive husband, Lionel. You never questioned my process. You never tried to discourage me. Instead, you gave me love, hugs, and a listening ear. I'm so grateful.

To my siblings: David, Herman, Wesley, Nicholas, and Isaac. I love you all immensely.

Dad, I thank you for giving me your blessing in writing this book. I love you so much box (inside joke). Lastly, and certainly not least, to my hero.

Words can't express my love for you and how much you have influenced almost everything that I do. I love you, Momma. Your legacy will live on through me, Linda Ann Patton.

Contents

•♡•♡•♡•♡•♡•

"… Our Father which art in heaven, Hallowed be thy name. Thy kingdom come. Thy will be done in earth, as it is in heaven. Give us this day our daily bread. And forgive us our debts, as we forgive our debtors. And lead us not into temptation, but deliver us from evil: For thine is the kingdom, and the power, and the glory, for ever. Amen."

Matthew 6:9-13

Memories

In 2019, I began to have memories of my childhood. They were violently invading the forefront of my mind. Certain smells, words, and environments would produce an extreme discomfort in my demeanor and disposition. I would find myself around certain individuals, and something within them would vex my spirit and would trigger me. It was familiar. Something that I thought I had run away from. Something that was hidden and deeply rooted to the core of me. Something that I never imagined that I would discuss, let alone, write about.

However, God has a way of using an available vessel to do exactly what He wants for His glory.

In mid-2022, I was sitting in my church praising and worshipping God. The service was close to ending, or so I thought. If you know anything about a holiness church, the spirit of God can take over at any moment to change the direction of the service. My pastor, Bobby Smith, who just so happens to be a true prophet; began to allow the Lord to use him in a mighty way. He began to pray over all of the children. God began to deal with him about the spirits of perversion, lust, and molestation. As he was praying over the children, his direction changed and the Holy Ghost inside of him began to speak to me.

He read my mail, speaking of some things that the Lord was revealing to him concerning my childhood. All I could do is weep. He not only spoke of what transpired, without going completely in depth, but he prophesied my freedom. This is why it is so important to be under the right leadership and those who walk in integrity, authority, and truth; because they can see and address what others cannot.

That day, something broke in me. I heard the voice of the Lord tell me to stop writing the book that I was working on at that time. He told me to begin to write a book on molestation —it would help many and set them free. I was shocked because this is a subject that I have never fully discussed with anyone, let alone family!

Truthfully, with the exception of my current church, I've never experienced real-life issues being addressed without being swept under the rug. How do I discuss what has never been discussed? And how do I effectively communicate when I have never been exposed to a community of communicators? These are just a few of the questions that riddled my mind, but I perceived that I must do something that has never been done in my family.

I began writing this book the latter part of 2022, and I completed it at the end of February 2023. The warfare that I have experienced in trying to release this book has been more than I can describe. Why has it taken me so long? Fear. I tried talking myself out of having it published. I even questioned myself, maybe God didn't mean 2023 when He told me to release it. But now is the time.

The Lord has forgiven me for my disobedience and has afforded me another opportunity to release what I've held so dear. It's **time to talk** about it!

If you're looking for a sign to heal, this is it. Allow your Unhealed heart to become healed from the molesting hands.

ONE

IT'S JUST INNOCENT

---

*M*y first kiss was with one of my cousins. I remember not wanting it, not desiring it, nor asking for it; but being surrounded by multiple family members, who had the same desire in their eyes of exploration and curiosity. I was one of a few girls amongst a plethora of boys and young men. I recall being locked in a room at my Auntie's place, and desperately trying to escape.

When you're of a certain age, it seems like boys and girls have the same amount of strength; however, there comes a time in life where growth spurts take place. You're no longer six or seven. I was no longer as strong as the boys. There were obvious changes. Their voices began to drop from high pitch to a lower octave. Some of their voices changed long ago because they were older than me, but I digress.

There was a clear difference. I began to start developing at 10. That's the age that I first had a menstrual period. My breasts started coming in at 11. I had an extremely small waist, but was very hippy like my mother, at least that's what I've been told. I didn't see myself in that way though, because I was a tomboy and grew up around a majority of boys. There were many around me that no longer saw the tomboy. They saw something that caused a sexual stir in their mind. It always begins in the mind; the day dreams, the role play in the mind, the desire that becomes rooted in the heart, and eventually the desire becomes stronger than common sense or will power. It woke up the beast in them.

·♥·♥·♥·♥·♥·

BACK TO MY AUNTIE'S PLACE. THE DOOR WAS LOCKED, and I was surrounded by cousins. Their strength was overpowering. I remember being slammed on to the bed, me trying to scream, but they would cover my mouth or play music to muffle the sound. I remember them covering my head with a thick cover. I remember there would be times that it would be so hard for me to breathe as my head was covered so tightly. I can recall that my arms would be pinned. I remember hands slowly caressing the outside of my shirt. I had a bra on, but I would feel the hands stroking the outside of my chest.

There was a conflict. My body began to feel things it never felt before, but this is family. One particular cousin began to lift up my blouse. I would wiggle my body, tried kicking, but the more I resisted, the more adamant they were to explore me. They successfully lifted my blouse and bra and began to suck and kiss private areas that had never been touched. They began to caress me below my waist and even blow their hot breath on my pants where my thighs would meet. The door banged and I could hear my Auntie asking, "Why is this door closed"? Everyone would scramble, pull the cover off of my head, and open the door. She peeked her head in the room suspiciously and then walked away. I would feel like a deer in headlights just trying to get my bearings and figure out what was happening. What changed?

I tried escaping during and after her leaving, but they would block my exit, and the doors were blocked, then locked again.

"Tanya, you're becoming pretty, and you honestly need to learn how to kiss. Let me teach you."

"*But I don't want to learn how,*" I responded. I would hear them say,

"I'm going to teach you anyhow."

I would see them whispering with one another, expletives escaping their lips in admiration.

> **"Tanya, your hands are so soft."**
> **"Tanya, your feet are so soft and pretty."**

This was so confusing, wrong, and embarrassing. Why was this happening to me? First, a boy at school had been literally trying to force me to do stuff I didn't want to do. I had to deal with an adult male who had climbed on top of me, another adult whom I trusted caressing my thighs when they were around. On to this point, certain cousins were grooming me to be their fantasy.

Who do I turn to? Who do I tell? These secrets were adding to my already crazy childhood.

It's just innocent though. Right?

TWO

HARD TRUTHS

J understand that the first chapter was a bit much, but the foundation must be laid. I need to be clear so that you know that I understand. I understand what some of you are currently going through, or have gone through in your past. Here are some hard truths. Many of you are holding onto or dealing with some family secrets. You may ask, why is that important and why are you addressing this now? The answer is simple. It's never too late to become free.

Many cultures, families, cults, religions, etcetera, have a code of secrecy. We never talk about what happened, but we will mention that *"There are family secrets."* Or you'll even go a little further by saying something like, *"If you only knew what I've been through..."* and yet, we tend to hold our truth hostage. **The secret begins to torment you**, and the truth can sometimes create embarrassment and shame. But does it ever make the perpetrators feel that way?

We even protect those who have harmed us. It seems like they live their life freely, yet there is so much reservation and protection that the victim tends to provide. So this leads me to ponder: Why does the victim live in bondage while the abuser is free? This is something that is not typically discussed, but it's necessary.

LET ME BE CLEAR, IF SOMETHING IS RESOLVED, discussed, forgiven, etcetera, then that's a powerful place of freedom. If they have admitted their wrong, have shown remorse, have repented, and you have forgiven them, you can move on and move forward with your life without looking back. If there has been no discussion, no resolution, no coming out, or release, then the time is now. The hard truth is, freedom can sometimes hurt.

Think of someone literally being held captive. Imagine them trying to literally break free from chains or even tight ropes. It takes physical strength, a change in perspective, a change in posture, and more than anything, there is a spiritual change that takes place within you that creates the momentum to break free.

With that being said, the process of becoming free can hurt. You risk being hurt more in order to become free, and you also risk hurting others (unintentionally) in order to gain your freedom. It's okay to be selfish from time to time. Especially if it means it draws you closer to being whole. Yes, it hurts first, but the lasting results are freedom.

WHAT HAPPENED TO YOU COULD HAVE EXPOSED YOUR flesh to something that it may like, even though it's wrong. This is another hard truth to realize. For an example, your uncle touched you in that private area. It's wrong, and you know it's wrong. You don't like him. You don't even love him. You hate him for what he's done to you! But now, you like the feeling that he has given you. You become addicted to the feeling.

I know that these are very hard truths. You may need to take a break or a moment to cry or even to compose yourself, but let it out. You didn't ask for this. Accept the fact that what happened changed you. But it didn't kill you.

REMEMBER THAT WE OVERCOME BY THE WORD OF others' testimony.

I pray that my testimonies give you the strength to overcome whatever you have faced.

THREE

SHAME

The definition of shame is, *a painful feeling of humiliation or distress caused by the consciousness of wrong or foolish behavior.*[1] As a child, there were so many moments where I had felt this pain. I also felt less than, and not worthy. Honestly, I felt embarrassed. Why did so many boys and men look at me in a sexual way? I was a child. Was this my worth? I somehow felt like it was my fault that they targeted me. The very thought was painful.

I remember going through years of elementary, middle school, and high school wearing baggy clothes or "boy clothes" just so that no one would notice me. I wanted to disappear. I wanted to be invisible.

---

1. Oxford Languages, s.v. "shame," accessed February 26, 2025, https://www.google.com/search?q=definition+of+shame

It still brings tears to my eyes for the younger Tanya who wanted to be loved, but not by predators, and surely not in the way that it was given. I wanted the love of a consistent, present father. I wanted the love of a mother who wasn't distracted and hurt. I wanted her to see that while the places that she would go might appear to be innocent, because it was family, were detrimental to me.

I was embarrassed. I was confused, filled with anxiety, and fear. *But I couldn't tell my mother that it was some of her family members that were molesting me.*

As a child, my mind took on more than it could handle, and there were moments where I thought of the impact situations would have on others, instead of the impact it would have on me. Instead of rushing to my mother to try and discuss these serious matters, I would think to myself, "Who will she be able to talk to after this", "Where is her safe place", "Who can she run to", and "Will I ruin things for her"? How could I tell her this when we barely knew how to effectively communicate with one another?

As time passed, I could tell her any and everything. But secrets have a way of becoming bigger, and shame has a way of holding you captive. I was strong-willed like my mother. I learned at an early age to "just deal with it" or "just suck it up," whatever *"it"* was. It wasn't fair that there was a girl inside of me that was dealing with extreme embarrassment.

I remember living in our old home at 21514 S. Reynolds Street. I can vividly recall many occasions from ages 8-10, going to our restroom and putting the latch on the bathroom door to lock the door. I looked at myself in the mirror with tears in my young eyes, and I begged God to take me away.

See, I learned to pray when I was child. I was what some may call a "pew baby." My mother was an Evangelist/Prophetess and my father a Prophet. Yet there were so many traumatic and confusing acts that had happened to me, or that I witnessed in my childhood, that I just wanted to disappear and sometimes die. I looked at myself in the mirror and asked God if he would take me to Heaven.

I told Him I hated my life. I told Him about all the people who touched me. I told Him how scared I was when mommy and daddy would fight. I shared with the Lord how much I missed my big brother Nicholas, who had died when he was just a teenager. I told him how lonely I was because at this point, all of my brothers had moved out of the house. I told the Lord how I felt like I was adopted, and how I didn't belong. I told Him, I hated it here.

Needless to say, God didn't give me what I wanted; however, He allowed me to go through the process so that I can share my experiences and testimonies with those who have been through something similar. When I was a teenager, I was the choir director of a choir at a small church back home.

We were invited to sing at a local Baptist church, as they requested that we participate in their program with two song selections. The elders were older men who sat in the front and side rows of the church. The choir did an excellent job and I was so proud of them. The following day, one of the members of the Baptist church, who just so happened to be one of my mom's old friends, came to our place. I remember sitting on the couch in the living room and she rolled her eyes at me. My mother asked her, what was her problem? She told my mother,

"You need to keep your daughter on a leash, Because she had all of the men lusting after her! Every time she rocked side-to-side while directing, they followed her hips."

I was mortified.

My motive was never to seduce anyone. Truth is, I still felt like an innocent kid. I'd never had a boyfriend or anything. I had been a victim of boys and men who were hellbent on contaminating my innocence. I remember still sitting on the couch with tears in my eyes. I recall my mother telling the woman, who was no longer her friend,

"Maybe you all should put your perverted men on a leash. Maybe they need to stop lusting after my 15-year-old daughter! She can't help the way that she's built. Maybe they're sick and need deliverance! So the next time you think it's okay to come to my house...."

Well you can imagine how the rest of that conversation went.

THE TRUTH IS, ONCE MY MOTHER WOULD DISCERN ANY threat against me, she would defend me until the very end. She did not play, and that's partially another reason why I didn't share all of the many things that happened to me. My mother didn't play, and someone would have to pay for doing this to her daughter. After my mother's old friend left our place, my mother looked me in the eyes and said, *"Baby, it's not you. It's them."*

I held onto those words because they were the truth, and I needed them. My mother, the defender. If only she knew the shame I had felt at that very moment. How do you function as a child riddled with shame?

I COULD NEVER UNDERSTAND BLAMING VICTIMS, BECAUSE they were victims. I grew up in a time where secrets are for the family and not for the world to see or hear. I grew up in a time where we don't say or do things in front of "mixed company," as we do not want to bring embarrassment or shame to the family. We had so many rules for everything except for protecting the helpless and innocent.

Shame.

Shame is the thing I felt when my mind goes back to that man climbing on top of me. He still had his jeans on, but his pants were unbuckled, and the zipper was down. He smelled funny. I remembered him smelling weird. The stench permeated through his pores.

What would possess you to climb on top of a little girl who was under the age of 10?

It's mind blowing how those who should feel shame, do not. I cry for that helpless little girl. No, I won't feel sorry for her or go into a place of, "Woe is me," but I mourn for the little girl who just wanted her close and extended family to be *normal*.

Now that I have found my words as an adult, I believe the word I was looking for is: **WHOLE.**

FOUR

LUST

*M*olestation has a way of changing you. It changes how you view the world and how you function. You may have once believed that life was nothing but rainbows, sunshine, and butterflies. But you quickly have a taste of your reality, and what life has to offer you, and suddenly life becomes cold. I was naturally loving and giving, and I was definitely a social butterfly. I loved people and I wanted to be friends with everyone, no matter the cost. However, I quickly became an introvert who trusted nothing and no one. I became mean and standoffish. **I was broken before I was ten years old.**

I started having what I considered at the time, weird and unique situations. At a very young age, I experienced a "visitor" at night. It used to torment me. I didn't know what it was at that time, but I did know that it was a spirit. It would hover over me at night. I would even feel and hear breathing that wasn't my own, and fear would grip me so that I would cover my head with my blanket.

This visitor used to take my breath away, and even lay heavily on top of me. Then it would pervert my dreams, and cause things to happen to me naturally. I felt like this spirit practically had control over me during the night. It followed me until my Senior year in high school. That year, I was so distracted by my mother's illness, that I didn't sleep. I was trying to cope with my mother going through chemotherapy for the second time, and later passing away in my bedroom two months after I turned seventeen years old. I was lost. I was broken. I wanted to die.

Fast forward to my freshman year in college. My college experience felt like people were there to "hook up," no one was there to learn. I quickly realized that I wouldn't be able to disappear there either. Lust is a very strong sexual desire. The Merriam-Webster Dictionary describes lust as an unusually intense or unbridled sexual desire; an intense longing. I suddenly became popular, kind of like the "it girl" for the wrong reasons. My figure became the topic of most young men, and some women. I was always feeling others' strong desire for me. There were no parents, no one to set boundaries or rules. Just a whole bunch of sexually charged teenagers and young adults, ready to explore.

I HAD STRAIGHT MEN, BISEXUAL MEN, LESBIANS, AND women who claimed they never been with a woman before who were extremely intrigued and fascinated by me. The more I tried to isolate myself, the more people would want to gain access to me. They thought I was mysterious, and truthfully, I was mourning the loss of my mother, my jacked up childhood, and the absence of my father throughout some of my younger years.

I'VE HAD A TOTAL OF THREE STALKERS IN MY LIFETIME, the first one when I was 18. How does this even happen? Lust. Perversion. You couple that with some other spirits and that equates to a disaster.

It wasn't until I was older that I realized a unique turn in my life. Wherever I go, I caused exposure of others motives and intent. Jealousy and lust were always at the forefront. My first boyfriend exposed me to so much. It was as if there was a sign on my forehead saying, "pick me". He was into extreme pornography and had been with multiple women at a very young age. With all the baggage I had, I fit perfectly into his dream girl idea. All of his friends boldly told him they wanted to be with me. He would prance me around like his little trophy. Lust followed me everywhere. Lust, obsession, and perversion would follow me everywhere I'd go.

They wanted my body, but no one saw Tanya.

THEY DIDN'T SEE THE LITTLE GIRL THAT WAS mishandled and abused, the one who didn't want to be intimate with anyone. The girl who wanted to rekindle her relationship with the Lord. The girl who wanted her mommy back. I was so lost. And honestly, I didn't know how to find my way back.

Don't get me wrong, eventually, I began to willingly participate in some acts, but I never sought men out. Lust spirits would always find me. I didn't understand that seeds were planted in my childhood that would ultimately determine how my young adulthood would go. Men and women had this odd obsession concerning me.

Now please don't take this as me bragging or being boastful. Listen from an open and unbiased mindset. Imagine me being your daughter, your sister, your friend, and now hear me say that both men and women had an obsession with me. Do you know how terrifying this was for me? Sure, I was raised with nothing but brothers, and I could tell them what's going on. But I knew them. They would "handle it" for real, and I didn't want that on my conscience, and truthfully, I never shared it with them because I couldn't bear losing one of them too.

I was tired of taking "L's."[1] I wanted happiness for myself and for my siblings. I wanted to win. I just didn't know how, because I couldn't identify the spirits that were working overtime to hold me back. The Bible says that,

"My people are destroyed for lack of knowledge..."—Hosea 4:6.

Knowledge is power and you certainly cannot expect to effectively fight without it. Well, I didn't know that lasciviousness had a grip on me. And I wasn't aware of strongholds, soul ties, incubus and succubus, generational curses, etcetera, so I was fighting a losing battle, not knowing enough to know what I was up against.

Truth is, you can't wish lust away. Some things literally come by fasting, praying, and therapy. I was swinging at an opponent that I could not see, in a fight I wasn't equipped for. All I knew is that I needed a big God to help me with these big problems.

Whew! I thank God for snatching me out of so many messes and sparing my life.

---

1. That's slang for "taking a loss."

FIVE

INCUBUS and SUCCUBUS

*I*n chapter four I mentioned that I used to have a "visitor" at night. This is where you're going to need your Bible so that you can see this for yourself; however, I will provide the scriptures for a quick reference. For those who don't know, the Bible was written by individuals that were INSPIRED by GOD, and that's why it's so important to read and study the word of God, because it's HIS word and He does not lie.

If you have endured or gone through molestation, rape, perversion and/or experienced sexual sins, you have now been exposed to certain demonic spirits.

Let's deal with these demons head on. The first chapter of Job in the Amplified Bible states this:

> Now there was a day when the sons of God (angels) came to present themselves before the Lord, and Satan (adversary, accuser) also came among them."

Job 1:6 AMP

NOW TURN TO THE SIXTH CHAPTER OF GENESIS. WE ARE going to look at the first five verses:

> Now it happened, when men began to multiply on the face of the land, and daughters were born to them, ²that the sons of God saw that the daughters of men were beautiful and desirable; and they took wives for themselves, whomever they chose and desired. ³Then the Lord said, "My Spirit shall not strive and remain with man forever, because he is indeed flesh [sinful, corrupt—given over to sensual appetites]; nevertheless his days shall yet be a hundred and twenty years." ⁴There were Nephilim (men of stature, notorious men) on the earth in those days—and also afterward—when the sons of God lived with the daughters of men, and they gave birth to their children. These were the mighty men who were of old, men of renown (great reputation, fame). ⁵The Lord saw that the wickedness (depravity) of man was great on the earth, and that every

imagination or intent of the thoughts of his heart were only evil continually."

Genesis 6:1-5 AMP

Pay close attention to verses 2 and 4. I gave you these scriptures to make it clear that in these particular passages, the *"sons of God"* are considered by a number of scholars and theologians to refer, not just to angels, but specifically to *fallen* angels. Clear enough, right?[1] You also read that they were attracted to and desired women, and became intimate with them. The Lord saw this wickedness, and later on, we read that He desired to destroy mankind because of all of the evil on the earth.

We know for certain that angels are spirits (see Hebrews 1:7, 14), which is why the second verse was able to differentiate "the sons of God" from "the daughters of men." There is a clear distinction between the two. We also know that these fallen angels desired daughters, women, or people in general and are not afraid to connect and contaminate them.

---

1. Some theologians reference five categories for "Sons of God." In these specific verses, they are using the Hebrew phrase *bene ha Elohim*, which is also used to refer to holy angels. See *"Sons of God,"* International Standard Bible Encyclopedia, ed. James Orr (Grand Rapids: Eerdmans, 1915), accessed May 7, 2025, https://www.biblestudytools.com/encyclopedias/isbe/sons-of-god.html.

Now that we have some scriptural backing, let's talk about what many have described as real-time encounters with demonic spirits—referred to in historical and spiritual writings by the names *Incubus* and *Succubus*.[2] These names come from ancient Mesopotamian and Sumerian lore, but were later integrated into Christian thought through the writings of figures like Augustine and Aquinas.

While the actual names, Incubus and Succubus were not mentioned in the Bible, the ideas and theories of Augustine and Aquinas supported the way many came understand certain night terrors, sexual torment, and spiritual oppression. This sparked interest, understanding, and debate throughout Church history. Whether these encounters stem from trauma or spiritual warfare, one thing is for sure: many have been tormented in the night and didn't know what to call it. If that's you, you're not alone—and it may be time to uncover what's really going on.[3]

---

2. The terms *Incubus* (from Latin *incubare*, "to lie upon") and *Succubus* (from *succubare*, "to lie beneath") originate from Roman usage but trace symbolically back to Sumerian myths of Lilu and Lilitu—spirits said to disturb humans at night. These names later appeared in Christian demonology and were associated with sexual visitations. See *Encyclopedia Britannica*, "Incubus," accessed May 9, 2025, https://www.britannica.com/topic/incubus; and *Etymonline*, s.v. "succubus," accessed May 9, 2025, https://www.etymonline.com/word/succubus.

3. Augustine discusses spiritual beings engaging in intercourse with women in *City of God*, Book 15, Chapter 23. Thomas Aquinas expands on this in *Summa Theologica*, I.51.3, explaining how demons may assume bodily form to interact with humans, contributing to the integration of these concepts

Have you ever:

Lay down while alone, and felt a presence near you or even hovering over you?

Experienced a sensual or sexual arousal that seems to manifest out of the blue?

Experienced an invisible caress that feels real, or even like your breath is being sucked or taken away?

Been asleep and all of a sudden, you begin to dream of sexual encounters? Has it ever felt so real that you experienced an orgasm in the dream?

Let's go a step further.

Have you ever experienced a real orgasm where no one is even touching you, as a result of a dream, intense imaginations, or an actual presence (not human)?

---

into medieval Christian thought. See Augustine, *City of God*, trans. Marcus Dods (New York: Modern Library, 1950), 15.23; and Thomas Aquinas, *Summa Theologica*, trans. Fathers of the English Dominican Province (New York: Benziger Bros., 1947), I.51.3, https://www.newadvent.org/summa/1051.htm.

If so, consider this: you may have encountered these real demonic spirits. You may even currently be experiencing some kind of torment or invasion while you sleep. I've said it once, but I'll say it again, we can be destroyed by what we do not know.

" My people are destroyed for lack of knowledge: because thou hast rejected knowledge, I will also reject thee, that thou shalt be no priest to me: seeing thou hast forgotten the law of thy God, I will also forget thy children."

Hosea 4:6

We Have Been Destroyed For A Lack Of Knowledge!

YOU CAN'T FIGHT WHAT YOU DON'T KNOW. NOW THAT WE know what we are up against, it's time to fight. Let me clarify: we must fight spiritually. How do we fight? We fight with the word of God. In the book of Isaiah we read:

> No weapon that is formed against thee shall prosper; and every tongue that shall rise against thee in judgment thou shalt condemn. This is the heritage of the servants of the LORD, and their righteousness is of me, saith the LORD."

Isaiah 54:17

That lets me know that there is nothing that satan or the fallen angels can do that can prosper as long as I'm in the will of GOD. The Bible also tells us:

> Put on the whole armour of God, that ye may be able to stand against the wiles of the devil. [12]For we wrestle not against flesh and blood, but against principalities, against powers, against the rulers of the darkness of this world, against spiritual wickedness in high places."

Ephesians 6:11-12

So, how do we fight? We are told to, *"Put on the whole armour of God, that ye may be able to stand against the wiles of the devil."* Spiritual armour are defensive tools utilized to defend or resist the enemy or satanic attacks. Why would we need to put on the armour? The same reason why a soldier would be expected to put on their whole armour for battle. **For**

Protection! When you are in a spiritual fight, you must be fully equipped with the whole armour of God to ensure that you are protected. What is the whole armour?

> Wherefore take unto you the whole armour of God, that ye may be able to withstand in the evil day, and having done all, to stand. Stand therefore, having your loins girt about with truth, and having on the breastplate of righteousness; and your feet shod with the preparation of the gospel of peace; above all, taking the shield of faith, wherewith ye shall be able to quench all the fiery darts of the wicked. And take the helmet of salvation, and the sword of the Spirit, which is the word of God: praying always with all prayer and supplication in the Spirit, and watching thereunto with all perseverance and supplication for all saints..."
>
> Ephesians 6:13-18

In addition to the above, the Bible says that some things come by fasting and praying, *"Howbeit this kind goeth not out but by prayer and fasting"* (Matthew 17:21 KJV).

FASTING HAS BEEN DESENSITIZED BY THIS GENERATION AS they now try to implement fasting in order to lose weight.

However, the initial purpose for fasting has a spiritual depth to it. If you need more information pertaining to fasting, I would like to encourage you to read Isaiah, chapter 58 and Matthew, chapter 6.

Read, study, and apply God's Word (The Holy Bible) and see that God will set you free from the bondage of wickedness.

> I declare and decree as God's prophet, that you will be completely delivered and set free from Incubus, Succubus, and all fallen angels that try to torment your dreams, your mind, your body, and your soul in Jesus' name.
> The blood of Jesus is against you, satan, and you are defeated in the mighty Name of Jesus!

Amen. Be free.

SIX

DISENGAGE

*A*ccording to the Oxford Languages Dictionary, the meaning of disengage is: ***to*** *separate or release (someone or something) from something to which they are attached or connected, to remove.*[1] After my mother died and I graduated from high school, I moved to another town to live with my paternal grandparents. I was a seventeen-year-old girl who was predominantly raised around my mother's side of the family. Now, I found myself spending most of my time around my father's family, whom I. had only seen occasionally.

Looking back, I can see how patient my grandparents were with me. They didn't just love my dad—their son—but they

---

1. Oxford Languages, s.v. "disengage," accessed February 26, 2025, https://www.google.com/search?q=definition+of+disengage.

also loved and adored my mother. I remember times I'd come home from school and my mother would mention that my grandparents had come by to visit her or to drop something off. They came to our upstairs apartment before my mom passed away, where she asked if they would take care of her "baby" (me). And after I graduated from high school, they did their best to do just that. I'm forever grateful. Still, I found it quite traumatic to experience such a drastic change at that age.

Under their roof, I learned and saw so many things that were foreign to me. My grandparents were also raising two other grandchildren, both being my first cousins, one of whom was my age and is also a girl. We talked about practically everything. We would even have sleepovers in each other's room. She would give me random hugs, which I found confusing at first. I thought it was different, but afterwards I learned she was showing me healthy love and affection between family. Her displays of endearment were pure towards me. Sometimes I didn't even know how to process this type of love from a cousin.

My grandparents hosted many family gatherings at their home and all of the Uncles, Aunties, and cousins exchanged hugs and kisses. Something as simple as seeing a cousin leaning their head on an Auntie's shoulder, and hearing them verbalizing their love for one another, changed my life. I watched them. I was accustomed to love looking very different, and at one point, all I wanted was to go back "home."

Real love shakes the foundation of fear and trauma. Sometimes **real love can feel like trauma when it contradicts your dysfunction.**

Read that again.

Real love gives revelation. It forces you to question what you've been receiving, right up until the point of your eyes being opened.

To clarify, my mother's family are a peculiar people. They are my family. They are me and I am them. They are strong, resilient people who love God, and their family. They've taken some blows and keep going. I love my family. My mother's siblings adored me and I loved and still love all of my Aunties and Uncles. I also had some cousins that I had healthy relationships with.

I even lived with my mother's first cousin directly after my mother's passing because I had to complete high school. She took care of me, and over the years, has watched over me in every stage of my life. To this very day, I consider her to be like my second mom.

WHAT I'M REFERENCING IS PAINFUL SITUATIONS THAT impacted *me*, that changed the trajectory of my journey, and caused me to fight for my life in ways that I wish I hadn't had to. It was because of these situations that I began to slowly disengage and detach myself from people, places, and things that created anxiety and reminded me of the molesting hands.

Family.

I do not mean that ALL of them had molested me. It could have been their son, their nephew, or their cousin who betrayed me *and* my mother's trust, because we thought I was surrounded by safe people and in safe environments.

Trauma has controlled me most of my life. I've been living in such a way that I allowed trauma to be swept and remain under the rug. Rather than to subject myself to certain things that would cause me more stress, I chose to disengage. I did it for myself. I did it for my peace of mind. I wanted to survive. Truthfully, I just wanted to forget.

BUT WHAT HAPPENS WHEN GOD HIMSELF PULLS THE RUG off from under you, and causes you to see all that has transpired? What happens when the things that your mind protected you from, resurfaces? God is revealing to many of us that it's time to deal with these things and go through the process. God is saying,

> It's okay, My child. Run into My loving arms for I will never leave you nor forsake you. Don't allow the hurt from your past to break you. You were built and created for this. You were built to be my example of an overcomer.
>
> Your testimony will cause many to draw strength and to no longer be captive to their past. Arise. Take up your bed and walk. For the time has come to be strong in the Lord and in the power of His might."

God said it, and I receive it.

SEVEN

TAKE THE LIMITS OFF

> Now to Him who is able to [carry out His purpose and] do superabundantly more than all that we dare ask or think [infinitely beyond our greatest prayers, hopes, or dreams], according to His power that is at work within us..."
>
> Ephesians 3:20 AMP

Why don't we operate in our greatest capacity? Oftentimes, we have allowed life, and the things that have been thrown at us, to change our natural state and structure. For example, as a survivor of molestation, I've learned how to cope, but not live. I trusted no one, and if

I can be honest with you, I still struggle with trust issues. There is a place of beautiful, pure wonder that a child maneuvers through that hasn't been altered, infiltrated, and contaminated by the world.

I RECENTLY SPENT A WEEK WITH MY 13-YEAR-OLD NIECE, Kira. There was such a beauty about her that only comes from being closer to your purest self. I heard it in her laughter, I saw it in her kind eyes, and I heard it in her voice when she said, "Thank you, Auntie." She was so unguarded and free. It was trust.

It made me want to protect her at all costs. I saw in her what I didn't see in myself. It was clear though, that her trust wasn't extended to everyone. However, there is an openness that I saw that I pray that she doesn't allow the world to take away from her. That openness is powerful.

My youngest niece, Talitha, is three years old. In her, I see unshakeable freedom in the purest form. No limits. No boundaries. I see it in her the most—the twinkle in her eyes when she gets away with absolutely everything, because she has her daddy wrapped around her beautiful, spoiled finger. LOL. One thing about me is I see practically everything. I recall a moment after church where Talitha had on her dress and twirled in circles. She was so carefree. She is free!

THIS IS WHAT GOD DESIRES FOR YOU. HE WANTS YOU TO take the limits off of your mind, your heart, your present, and your future. He wants you to experience true freedom. He does not want you to be bound by your past or your present. He yearns to do exceedingly abundantly ABOVE all that we ask or think; however, we no longer believe this, *because we are no longer free.*

He wants you to twirl again.

· ♥ · ♥ ∘ ♥ ∘ ♥ · ♥ ·

IMAGINE THAT EVERY YEAR OF YOUR LIFE, YOU ACQUIRE A new piece of luggage that you have to carry. Imagine being in your 30s, 40s, and even older, carrying 40 backpacks that are filled with mess. Or even worse, you have 50 pieces of luggage filled with junk and have absolutely no help carrying the load. That's what you're doing now. Every year that you don't deal with whatever has transpired, you add on another piece of luggage that you have to carry. Can you imagine the toll that it takes on you to carry such heavy weight on a regular basis?

Sometimes, I fill my purse with so much stuff that it causes me to lean to one side. It changes how I walk and it literally shifts my posture. That's what's happening with many of us now. We've carried so much that now we're hunched over. Our natural state has been altered. Our backs are curved, our chest is caved in, our shoulders are weighed down to the ground, our fingers and hands are calloused, our sight has declined, our skin has cracked, and our legs are about to cave from the heaviness. Yet we're wondering why we can't achieve our visions.

We're befuddled at our lack.

GOD IS SAYING,

"No more. Take the limits off so that I can prove to you that I am God. Take the limits off so I can help you reach you greatest potential. Come back to Me, your first love, where it all began. I created you with a purpose, and because of this world's imperfections, it changed you. Let Me help you to be who I created you to be. Allow My thoughts of you to take precedence over your fears and doubts. It is time to heal."

EIGHT

RELAPSE

There are moments in recovery—or in trying to overcome an addiction—when it may feel like your life and everything in your world is getting worse. It's as if you take one step forward only to be knocked back ten. But this struggle isn't unique to addiction. Maybe you've faced domestic violence, betrayal, parental abuse, or abandonment. Whatever your experiences are, there are times when you feel like you finally have a handle on everything. You go about your day, consumed with life. Your work, spouse, children, friends, church, or social gatherings create the illusion that your life is not only full but complete.

WE FILL OUR SCHEDULES AND OUR MINDS WITH distractions, avoiding the inner enemy. Often, we do this unintentionally. Sometimes, we do it intentionally. We call it coping. But mostly, it happens because we were never taught how to face things head-on. Yet, life has a way of reminding you of what hasn't been processed. More importantly, in order for you to reach your greatest potential, God will expose the areas that require more work.

Let me speak to this.

Have you ever started doing the work on yourself—getting through the minutes, managing the hours, building confidence as the days pass—thinking to yourself, *I got this*? Then... BOOM! A smell, a touch, a conversation, a building, or even a person **triggers** you. Just when you're trying to heal a wound, it feels like someone is ripping the scab off prematurely, and now you're bleeding again. Back to square one.

I've been there.

The tears flow. Or maybe you fall back into old habits—doing what you did before to mask or cope with whatever demon you're wrestling with. You forget the tools you learned because you're still new to this healing process. You feel disappointed that the pain still lingers, and discouragement creeps in. You run back to that drug, that unhealthy relationship—you return to the very detrimental thing that caused harm in the first place. However, in that moment, you don't see it that way.

My old vice? E&J mixed with a little bit of orange juice—and sometimes, an ex. That one thing would lead to another and before I knew it, the cycle I had worked so hard to break was again within arm's reach. And just like that, I was adding to my own toxic story of abuse and hurt. Sabotaging my whole process. **Relapsed!**

A deterioration after a period of improvement. A return to a less active, or worse state.

How did we get here?

Did I mention before that I'm an extremist? When I did good, I did *real* good. But when I did bad? I went all out —I did my very best at being bad, with my bad self. Forget all the hard work of "taking the limits off" like the last chapter encouraged. I'd go from zero to one hundred in seconds.

And then, reality sets in. When you sober up from the sex, drugs, bad relationships—or whatever your *thing* is—you realize what you've just done. Now, you're back with that old demon called **shame**.

Understand this: **healing is a process.** No one said the road would be easy. You've dealt with years of turmoil—it's time to give yourself some grace. Yes, you relapsed. But after a relapse comes your opportunity for a fresh start. Now is the time to recover.

There is nothing too bad that God can't help you to fix. *You will not die here.* Dust yourself off and keep it moving. Who cares who watched you fall?

The Bible says,

> ...for all have sinned, and come short of the glory of God..."

Romans 3:23

That lets me know that none of us have arrived. We have all fallen short. What's most important is *not to stay there*.

Make it up in your mind that it is all working out for your good, that means even your mistakes can be turned into something positive.

> And we know that all things work together for good to them that love God, to them who are the called according to his purpose."

Romans 8:28

If you love God, and you continue to strive to do God's will, even your mistakes can work together for your good.

Just don't stay there.

Don't stay in that mess.

Don't stay in that rut.

Don't feel sorry for yourself.

Pick yourself up and try again.

There is more for you to accomplish. You are on the brink of a **complete breakthrough**.

NINE

RESENTMENT

This chapter is a big one. I have never released how much I've resented several individuals for what I went through as a child. Interestingly enough, the perpetrators were not on the top of my list of people that I resented. Please hear me. Truthfully, I do hold those who hurt me responsible for their actions. However, I don't deal with them in any capacity that would hold any weight concerning me. They were definitely on the list, but those I resented the most are the people you may have least expected.

During my childhood, my parents fought a lot, which resulted in many separations. My mom would take me, and all of my brothers would be with our dad. There is a level of hurt and resentment that I had toward my parents that I have not been able to articulate until this very moment. For years, I was so angry at my Dad, although I never told him how I felt; because then I would have to face my feelings and explain to him why I felt the way that I did. You see, as I'm writing this chapter, he still doesn't know that I was molested and mishandled by many.

Eventually, my parents divorced. I was around eleven or twelve, living permanently with my mother for the remainder of her life. Although my dad would send me letters and money throughout my early and teenage years, I could count on one hand how many times I saw him. While I want to provide some clarity about the family dynamics so my perspective as a child can be understood, I won't go any further into that or my parents relationship.

SOMEHOW, I WOULD FIND MYSELF IN SITUATIONS WHERE I was surrounded by perversion. The first couple incidents, my first thought was, *"Where is my Daddy?"* A few other traumatic events occurred and I would, *"wish my Daddy was here to protect me."* There were many moments I convinced myself that if I had lived with my Dad, or if he was around, I wouldn't be at the hands of those who felt free to fondle or tamper with my innocence, because my Dad was a protective and intimidating man.

GROWING UP, MY DAD WAS LARGER THAN LIFE. NO ONE was as strong, as intimidating, or as masculine in my book. He could beat up any bad guy and every boogeyman. He was a man's man. My mind couldn't comprehend why he couldn't be that for me in the time that I needed him the most.

Somehow, I would find myself in situations where I was surrounded by perversion. The first couple of incidents, my first thought was, *"Where is my Daddy?"* A few other traumatic events occurred, and I would think, *"I wish my Daddy was here to protect me."*

There were many moments I convinced myself that if I had lived with my dad, or if he was around, I wouldn't be at the hands of those who felt free to fondle or tamper with my innocence, because my dad was a protective and intimidating man.

You can imagine the hurt and disappointment I experienced the times when there were promises made to pick me up, but it never happened. I recall multiple times when my luggage was packed, and I would sit outside on the front porch steps, waiting until the sun went down.

Tears would mist my eyes, and my vision would become foggy. I can hear my mother now: *"Tanya Ann, get in the house. He's not coming."* I would stomp my feet all the way to my bedroom and throw myself on the bed.

I wasn't just disappointed and hurt. I was trying to find an out. I needed an escape, even if it was just temporary. Yes, him not showing up was devastating all on its own. I learned not to trust his word in those pivotal moments.

But it wasn't just the "no-shows." It was the fact that I felt he would leave his *"favorite and only daughter"*—as he used to call me—in compromising situations. Where was my protection? Where was my safe haven? He was the leader of our pack, and in my young mind, he left his baby girl uncovered.

I blamed him. If I'm honest, at the time, I blamed him more than I blamed my mother. From my twelfth to eighteenth years, more than ever, I needed to see how a man was supposed to treat a woman. I needed an example. I also needed to know and feel the protection of my father.

Yes, I have Daddy issues.

But how can one acknowledge or even repair what they don't know is broken? Sadly, he doesn't even know it. However, I am going to remedy that. **There's freedom in being honest.**

MY DAD AND I ARE SO CLOSE NOW, BUT I HAVE FAILED him. I have not given him the opportunity to know, process, and understand what I went through in those years. It's a disservice to him and to our relationship.

For me, even in our closeness, there is a part of me that holds that piece of my life close to my chest. I have protected my past like I would protect my child. I have safeguarded so much information out of fear that my vulnerability would be exposed.

I don't know about you, but if you've ever been the "strong one" in your family, there's an expectation. People often glamorize that title as though it is some elite thing. In all actuality, sometimes it is a façade that prevents many from true healing. The Bible says, *when I'm weak, he makes me strong* (Joel 3:10 paraphrase). Why is there so much shame attached to our weakness?

Let me free you today. Having a weakness is not a weakness. It is a sign that you are human and have room for improvement. It causes us to walk in humility and realize that we cannot do it all on our own, or with our own power. We need our great big God to help us. **Resentment** is bitter indignation at having been treated unfairly.

I resented my mother. As I became older, my mother and I became closer; however, there was a period of time, when I was between five and thirteen years old, we did not communicate as we should. I didn't think my mother liked me for a very long time. I recall telling her, *"I'm going to make you love me."* That gives you an idea of how I believed my mother felt concerning me. The truth is, my mother loved and adored me and raised me the best that she could, but I was unable to see that until I became older.

Through those early years, there were many distractions that created division, and so the healthy dynamics of a mother-daughter relationship did not develop until my later years in high school. How do I tell this strong woman, this evangelist, this prophetess, the one that everyone looked up to and called mother (which I couldn't understand at that time), the one that brought everyone together, that I was being molested? How do I tell her that I was receiving more attention than I had ever received in my life? And that it was bad?

So, I resented her for putting me in a position where I didn't feel safe enough to speak during those early years, which carried over into my teenage years. Now don't get me wrong, I literally told my mother EVERYTHING when I became a teenager, as our relationship flourished beautifully. I told her everything, *except* for my hidden shame of being touched, fondled, and abused by some strangers, and even those that she loved.

I wondered how she was able to see everything but that, although I've since let that portion of resentment go. No longer do I resent my parents for being so distracted with each other that they couldn't see that their baby was hurting. I had to release that not only for them, but for myself. Truth is, they did their best as parents and I wouldn't trade them in for the world. I love both of them equally and I honor them. To this day, I do things with them in my mind as I want to make them proud.

I've learned that holding resentment causes sickness, illnesses, and sometimes death. It kills you like cancer. It is dangerous and you tend to hurt yourself more than anyone else. Resentment punishes the host and can destroy your life. Say this with me:

> I release resentment. Resentment, you no longer have power over my mind, body, or soul. I rebuke the spirit of resentment, bitterness, and unforgiveness and I cast it to the pit of hell. I will now walk in freedom, love, and forgiveness in Jesus' name. Amen."

You're now free from resentment.

Believe and receive it.

TEN

I TOLD HIM

*E*veryone has their own process and way of processing trauma. I've seen those who have confronted their abuser(s) head on, and they felt liberated. Confronting an abuser in hopes of resolve is not wrong. I've also seen some who have written letters to their abuser(s) in order to feel the freedom that they need, also not wrong. I'm a bit different.

My concern is not my interactions with my abusers as they no longer hold any power in my life. This is not to diminish those who feel that they need to process in that way, it's just not the way the Lord has led me.

Personally, I don't need their apology and I don't need them to hear my side of the story. They were there. Whether they were an adult or a juvenile when the abuse took place, time has passed. They are now all adults who are aware of their past actions. My healing is not predicated on their actions or lack of actions. My journey to wholeness includes making things right amongst those that are in my inner circle. They are the ones who truly matter to me. This is my journey and I'm not wrong.

I've shared, in small increments, minimal information to my siblings relating to the molesting hands. I've given no names, I have not provided detailed information, and I've operated this way for protection purposes. I adore all four of my living brothers, and because I love them and they love me, wisdom says to "protect their hearts". We've gone through so much. All of my brothers could literally write bestselling novels because the things that they have gone through are unimaginable. They are the true MVP's.

Moreover, I would never want to cause heartache or even a divide among family, so I choose both to be honest and to use wisdom. It's my choice and I choose peace. Because they love me, I know that they will respect and honor that.

• ♡ • ♡ • ♡ • ♡ • ♡ •

I TOLD HIM. IT WENT A LITTLE SOMETHING LIKE THIS. I was at his place and we were facing each other and I said, "Dad, can I talk to you about something". Now after reading chapter 9, you can imagine why this conversation is so crucial. I heard him say, "Sure daughter". "Dad, I would never say anything to hurt you. I've put off having this conversation for long enough. God has a way of bringing things to the surface, and as a result, I'm writing a book about molestation". He slowly nodded. Digesting every word that I say. It was almost as if I could see his mind processing. He replies "Okay". I pause and he says, "you can continue".

With glossy eyes, I hear myself say "Dad, I was molested multiple times by multiple people..." and at this point the tears are now streaming down my face, but more than ever, I'm intentional about my words. I know what needs to be said and it has to be done. I speak slowly and clearly to ensure that every word was understood. I didn't go into the gory details, and no names were mentioned, but I knew with each word that I was gaining strength. I felt empowered. More than anything, I felt true release in all capacities breaking forth.

What was so beautiful about this moment, my dad ushered me through each minute, lovingly. He was selfless. He was caring and understanding. He took responsibility for not being more aware of my surroundings and the conditions that I was in. Though the molestation happened years ago, he reassured me that my feelings were valid as a child and even as adult. That reassurance is everything to a daddy's girl. The love of a father to a girl, is something that a daughter will never forget, be it good or bad; and at that moment, as grown as I am, I needed it.

I made it clear that I wanted to make him and my mommy proud and he told me that he was and he knew that my mother would be as well. I explained to him how the Lord told me to write a book concerning this subject as there was a true need for ideas and strategies of overcoming certain demonic forces, etcetera. Just like the true man of God that he is, he said "God said it, Daughter. DO IT". I cried. I wasn't able to have this conversation with my mom, but I know her. She would have said, "Baby, let the Lord use you." And that's what I intend on doing. I told HIM. My Daddy. And it freed me.

I'm so grateful for being able to document my journey concerning the molesting hands. Lord knows, things got worse during this process, before they got better. But anything worth having is worth fighting for, right?

Fight for your freedom. Fight for your deliverance. Fight for your peace of mind. One day, you won't have to fight anymore. You will be dwelling in peace that surpasses all understanding, and you'll think back and remember that time when things were dark. You'll say to yourself, only God could have given me this type of peace.

Now breathe!

Freedom looks good on you.

To You, Dear Reader

I want to encourage every reader to do something that they haven't done before. Take a moment to reflect on what is holding you back. What's keeping you from going after your dreams or achieving a goal? Oftentimes, there are things from our past that are influencing our decisions in our present and in our future. What are you afraid of? What's stopping you? I admonish you on today, to dismantle the lie that you've accepted. Free yourself from doubt, shame, rejection, and fear.

Listen, it would be a shame to be gifted with no release. You've been carrying it for so long. My brave brother, my beautiful sister...there is hope. You can and you will do this. The hardest part of change, is taking the first step. It won't always be comfortable, but best believe that it is leading you to a better you.

Remember, you are not alone. Be kind to yourself. Be gentle. You know what being mishandled feels like. Don't go back to that place or space. Allow yourself to feel love. Embrace it. Love yourself enough to be whole. Take that exercising class. Read or write that book. Start that business. Go back to college. Finish what you've started and breathe again. You can do it.

It's never too late to become a solution.

I BELIEVE IN YOU!

Let Us Pray...

First, I want to spend some time to say, "Thank you." Thank you , Jesus, for your goodness and mercy. Thank you for your loving kindness and faithfulness. Thank you for never leaving us or forsaking us. Thank you for keeping us safe from all hurt, harm, and danger. We thank you for searching our hearts and cleansing us from things that displease you. Thank you for birthing something new within us. We repent and ask that you forgive us for all of our sins and unrighteousness. We understand that you have thoughts concerning us so we submit to your will and your way. We trust your plans. We commit to casting all of our cares and all of our burdens on you, for you truly care for us. Give us the mind of Christ and give us the will to change. Provide us with resources, blueprints, and plans to press towards the right direction.

Show us how to execute the plans and steward well over all that you have blessed us with. Satan, the Lord rebukes you right now in the name of Jesus. We rebuke the spirit of fear, anxiety, doubt, shame, confusion, perversion, and even suicide in the name of Jesus. We cancel every spirit of rage, depression, pride, and strife. We pull down every heavy weight and every stronghold and cast it to the pit of hell, never to return. We thank you Jesus for peace that surpasses all understanding. We decree and declare that you are our Lord and Savior. We decree and declare that we are the head and not the tail, above not beneath, a lender and not a borrower. We thank you for giving us authority to tread our feet on the enemies head. We know that no weapon that is formed against shall prosper. We walk in the full armor of God.

Thank you for Holy Ghost power. We thank you that you have created in us a new heart and renewed the right spirit within us. We thank you for true deliverance and wholeness. We love you, Lord. We will never be the same again. In the matchless name of Jesus Christ, so be it unto us. Amen.

About The Author

The daughter of preachers, Tanya Jefferson grew up in both, a small town and in the city. Growing up, she moved frequently as life was a bit unstable. She acquired her love for literature through her mother, as she would take her to the public library once a week. As time progressed, Tanya realized that she loved reading and writing. It was a place where she could disappear, or travel through her imagination by way of the words that were written on the pages of each book.

Tanya was twice approached in high school to have a poem and a story that she had written published; however, due to her mother's illness, she declined multiple times. After her mother's passing, her enthusiasm to write slowly vanished. For years, she put off the inevitable.

Now happily married, a believer and minister of Jesus Christ, she understands that now is the time to release what God has prompted her to share. Time to write the testimony, provide the tools, and knowledge obtained throughout the years in order to heal, deliver, and set free. Join her on this wonderful journey. The journey of the writer, the scribe.

Coming Soon From Tanya Jefferson

Stay tuned for *Unhealed Heart, The Book of Jealousy*, the next *Unhealed Heart* installment.

www.ingramcontent.com/pod-product-compliance
Lightning Source LLC
Chambersburg PA
CBHW071110090426
42737CB00013B/2553